# SONATA
## *for* VOICE *and* SILENCE

# SONATA
## *for* VOICE *and* SILENCE

MEDITATIONS

Mark Belletini

SKINNER HOUSE BOOKS
BOSTON

Printed in the United States

Cover design by Kathryn Sky-Peck
Text design by Suzanne Morgan
Cover photograph *Hush* © 2003 Elena Kachuro-Rosenberg,
http://elenarosenberg.com/

ISBN 1-55896-536-X
978-1-55896-536-2

6  5  4  3  2  1
11  10  09  08

Library of Congress Cataloging-in-Publication Data

Belletini, Mark.
  Sonata for voice and silence : meditations / Mark Belletini.
      p. cm.
  ISBN-13: 978-1-55896-536-2 (pbk. : alk. paper)
  ISBN-10: 1-55896-536-X (pbk. : alk. paper)  1. Unitarian
Universalist churches—Prayers and devotions. 2. Spiritual
life—Unitarian Universalist churches--Meditations. 3. Public
worship—Unitarian Universalist churches—Meditations.  I. Title.

BX9855.B45 2008
242—dc22

                                        2007047511

# CONTENTS

III  ELEGIES

IV  FINALE

# 1    PRELUDE

Although R. Waldo Emerson famously said he liked "the silent church before the service better than any preaching," my experience is that most congregations are known more for their words or music than the quality of their quiet.

Yet sounds are actually rare in the vast cosmos which holds our lives. Silence surrounds the farthest star and the nearest. Our planet itself is swathed in silence save within its thin skin of air. Moonlight makes no sound; sunlight falls through the air quietly. The night side of the earth is largely silent. Silence bathes what happened before us, and what shall follow us.

Thus, a time of silence during an ordered span of worship may  serve as a communal emblem which reminds us that we are part of a vast silent reality, part of each others' lives, at one with the silent flow of past into future through the gate of the present moment.

Of course, silence can be used as an emblem of domination and irresponsibility. Some families, corporations, or even congregations can keep a destructive and painful silence about realities that still seem to hurt everyone—involved or not involved. This is why during worship I use prayer to make clear what kind of silence is being invoked. I don't call for the silence which hurts, but for a tender silence emblematic of health, wholeness, communion, care, and humility. A silence that ties us inextricably as much to each other as to far galaxies.

I hope these prayers evoke our certain connections to the world, to each other, and to that nameless Depth which, with a host of modern poets, I simply call Love. There may appear to be a variety of theological viewpoints expressed in these prayers, these sequences, as I call them on Sundays. I assure you, each of these viewpoints courses through my mind, my heart and my imagination daily. Like the various themes of a sonata, they weave into a singular whole, supported by the rhythm of my heart and flicker of my dreams.

The third section consists of seven prayers written for an individual, my beloved mentor, Harry Scholefield. Few things in my life have so deeply moved me as Harry's request that I write a book of prayers to help him come to terms with the end of his life. The book reflected my visits with him, when we would often read or recite prayer-poems together. In his final days, when he was no longer in his own home, he and his wife Diene read prayers from the book I wrote for him, two every day. These are prayers with specific biographic details, but they invite personal meditation on that final safe and silent mystery which will greet us all at last.

The finale depicts the vision of a healed social world, which is the vision of hope I shared with Harry, and which, with the grace of silence, strengthens my ministry.

It is to the continuing presence of both Harry and Diene that I dedicate this Sonata for Voice and Silence.

# II  PRAISES

## Reading for the Day

Let the sky above me unroll like a scroll,
and let me read upon it today's text for my life:
　　"You are alive, here and now.
　　Love boldly and always tell the truth."

Let the wind arrange the naked branches
of the maples and aspens and oaks
into letters which proclaim this sacred text:
　　"Your heart beats now,
　　not tomorrow or yesterday.
　　Love the gift of your life and do no harm."

Let the eyes and hands and faces
of all men and women and children
with whom I share this earth
be chapter and verse in this great scripture text:
　　"Life is struggle and loss, and also
　　tenderness and joy.
　　Live all of your life, not just part of it."

And now let all the poems and scriptures and novels
and films and songs and cries and lullabies and
prayers and anthems open up before our free hearts.
Let them open like a torah, like a psalm, like a gospel,
like an apocalypse
and let them proclaim:

> "Do not think you can take away
> each other's troubles,
> but try to be with each other in them.
> Remember that you are part, not all,
> great, but not by far the greatest,
> small, precious brief breaths
> in the great whirlwind of creation."

And remember that every single human word is
finally and divinely cradled in the strong and secure
arms of Silence.

## ANOTHER PSALM 139

To be present to the life of this place,
and to the deep that calls unto deep,
it matters only that we know there is no place
to flee from what presents itself to us here.
We can imagine flying to dark green islands
far away in a teal sea bronzed by sunset,
but still the questions and answers

will dance within us, knock at our doors,
haunt us in the dark.
We can imagine pulling up the corner
of the autumn morning sky,
and slipping away into a place too strange to name,
but still the questions and answers will glide within us,
pound on our doors, call to us in the dark.
We can imagine running away
to the dark side of the earth,
where spices float in the rivers
and children nurse at midnight breast,
but still the questions and answers
will circle within us, rap at our doors,
and touch our shoulders in the dark.
For there is no place to flee from the presence
that presents itself here, the face we each recognize
in the mirror of our lives, the yearning that is the
breath in our own breath.
Flee to the presence, or stay here for it. It makes no
difference
for we are here, present to what presents itself to us.
Welcome.
Welcome to the silence.

## During Wartime

One day, I pray,
in clear and clean windows,
reflections of families at supper,
not mouths open in fear.
One day, I pray,
in wide hot streets,
clean air, not belching oily smoke.
One day, I pray,
on warm spring nights,
the sound of crickets, not wailing or gunshots.
One day, I pray,
in human hearts,
a prayer of thanksgiving for a peace that
has lasted a hundred years;
not a truce, mind you,
but an Era of Peace full and rich and just.
May our children live to see such a world,
O Love, may all children live.
What indeed can we do?
We can breathe. We can feel heartache.
We can breathe. We can be loyal to spring.
We can breathe. We can remember the
difference between what we can do
before we have thought
and what we can do after we have thought.
We can breathe. We can remember the ways

our feelings can serve our mind.
We can breathe. We can refuse to sign
our lives over into the service of panic
or hand-wringing self-righteousness.
We can breathe. We can get clear on our
most basic values. We can breathe.
Blest are you, breath, for you are
the spirit that sustains me in difficult days.


## TOGETHER

Here we are together in this great room.
We are all under the many warm colors
braiding through the wood in the ceiling.
We are all above the carpet enriched with
turquoise and red.
Together we can note the green plants up front
which came from lands far away.
Together we can note shuttered windows
opening up onto the local day;
together we can slowly breathe in the air
which yesterday wafted over the Rockies,
and tomorrow will arch over Labrador.
In the air, molecules and atoms and empty space,
molecules and atoms and emptiness
which once may have been part of the hand

which the Dutch heretic Spinoza called his own,
and another atom of air may have been breathed
by Buddha's wife over the crib of their son,
and still a third may have been part of the
wooden house in Chicago where Jane Addams
sat down to read the text in the gospel:
"Blessed are you poor."
The whole history of the world
is in this room,
not just by the imagination of the human heart,
but by the revelation of the physicist and statistician.
Thus, this is indeed a sacred place.
But no more sacred than everything outside
its louvered doors, from the Memorial Garden
ten meters from this pulpit
to the star Epsilon Eridani ten light years away,
a beautiful star which itself is washed in a silence
much like this.

## DE COLORES

All the colors make a world, O Truth.
You are none of them and yet all of them.
All of them.
Hand the color of wheat joined
to hand the color of cream tea.

All of them.
Eyes dark as maple bark and
light as glacier ice.
All of them.
Torsos cinnamon and caramel and cocoa,
foreheads reflecting the blue of the noon sky
or rust of the sunset.
All of them.
The chartreuse of leaves drooping
off winter rhododendrons in the sun,
the restrained gray of stone,
and thickets of branches the color of cola.
All of them.
The white of snowflakes, the pewter clouds,
the black wrought iron railings on porches...
every shade and tint and hue make a world.
Mahogany arms and shoulders the color of rain
puddles,
indigo evenings and pale saffron dawns,
all the hues of rage or despair,
all the colors shimmering in musical chords,
all the shades of silence,
they are you, O Truth, they are you,
far more than these flimsy and tissue-thin words.

## SLOWER AND SLOWER

Let the difficulties of the week
take their sabbath now,
their brief and simple rest.
Let the worries of the week
lay their heft gently onto the dark earth
below this carpeted floor
which can bear them with greater ease
than any one of us can by ourselves.
Let the tangle of feelings,
the pull and push of these last seven days
sit still for a minute,
stop writhing in my heart,
and move no more than a Buddha
at rest under a tree.
Let there be stillness in my heart for a moment,
the balance point between breathing in
and breathing out, like the pause of a dancer
between movements in the music.
Let the breathing in this room be free and flowing.
Let pulses trance a slower rhythm in the wrist.
Let the coming silence be like hands
pulling back a curtain,
revealing the table set with the feast of life
which is present here and now
and has been the whole while,
present to those who give up living in either the past
or the future.

## ALWAYS THERE

Stars of twilight,
the gray clouds only hide you.
They do not steal you away.
You still burn there
on the dark mantle of infinity,
regardless of how anything obscures you.
You are neither impatient nor resentful.
You are just there, burning bright,
that I might grow as faithful.
Dreams of my mind,
nothing can take you away.
Dreams of children at play,
dreams of lovers holding hands in the streets,
dreams of friends embracing warmly,
dreams of families round the world
laughing at supper,
and dreams of a good day's work
and peaceful rest,
you continue to warm me
even when the nightmare of war
chills my heart.
You are there, oh dreams,
shining, warming,
regardless of how anything obscures you.
You are neither invalidated nor discountable.
You are just there, burning bright,
that I might be illumined.

Silence in my soul.
You too are always there,
hidden behind a thousand sighs
and a thousand clamoring headlines.
You often hide yourself under piles of snow,
you string yourself between bare branches,
you hover over the stars of twilight
and the dreams of my mind.
But, now, come out into the open, O Silence,
into this place and this hour, amid these people,
that we might be comforted and set free for a time.


## Via Negativa

Not the silence of a child finally asleep in a crib—
not the silence of pear blossoms falling—
not the silence of singers after the song—
not the silence of embarrassed strangers—
not the silence of streets when gunshot stops—
not the silence of rage—
not the red-faced silence of frustration—
not the silence of the exhausted—
not the silence of the gardener gardening alone—
but this:
the silence of those who have been together
and do not need to hide their aloneness with words,
the silence of lovers

who have come to a place of quiet comfort,
the silence of a newborn at breast,
the silence of an overflowing human heart
under the stars at night,
the silence of friends holding still
in a long and tender embrace.


## WAR REQUIEM

In the city of Yerevan, Mikael Alegezian, age 30,
names aloud the names of his great grandparents,
who died in the days
which reddened the hopes of Armenians
at the beginning of the last century.

In Liege, Belgium, Jean Saint-Jerome, aged 45,
gazes at the portrait of his great grandparents,
who perished near Maastricht
during the First World War.

In Piotrkow, Poland, Julia Czeskowic, age 90,
visits the grave of her parents in the village cemetery.
They were civilians, killed during the Second World
War when they refused to tell where their friends,
the Ginzbergs, were hiding.

In Kyoto, Japan, Tetsuji Yamamoto, age 88,
looks at the faded black and white photo

of his first young wife, Sumiko,
who had been visiting her aunt in Nagasaki
on that fateful day in August.

In Seoul, Korea, Kim Jun Ji, 78,
shuffles letters from his American pen pal
George Blanchard, who died in a rice field in his own
country almost six decades ago.

In Mt. Sterling, OH, Pete Henderson, age 53,
remembers the singular laughter of his red-headed
younger brother, which was silenced near Saigon so
many decades ago.

A time for memorial it is,
a time for remembering
the human loss in human wars, the silence of voices,
the bending of hearts forever.
We remember, we do not deny all these things
happened, we remember, and join our silence to the
silence of those who perished in wars, in skirmishes,
in revolutions, in revolts, in assaults, in riots, be they
civilians, or soldiers,
or human beings of any sort
caught up in the tangle of the years.
For all losses are real losses
to those whose love has not grown thin and sour.
And may all those who live be deepened
by their remembering in this silence.

## Sunday Spell

And now, with the striking of this bell,
it is all transformed.
Like wizardry.
Like magic.
Something like abracadabra,
but without the rabbits
or infinitely deep black hats.
The transformation is almost upon us.

Time measured by the hands of clocks
is now changed into time measured by breath,
in and out, in and out.

Time measured by memories and worries,
is now changed into time crafted
by the next heartbeat and the next.
Time's shadow stretching on a sundial
now changes into time's unsurpassed brightness
shining on the present second.

It's almost here,
a magic trick no different
than the first second of creation.
I am pulling the curtain back.
I am turning the card.
Look, it's the one you guessed.

## WORLDPRAYER

A typical week.
Near Chendu in China,
blue summer lupine stalks
continue to blossom in high meadows.

In Yozgat, Turkey, women put mint
into their eggplant as their husbands
play backgammon down at the café.

In Chamayo, New Mexico,
Diné fathers teach their sons
their Navajo heritage and language
under blue skies.

In Baghdad and Jerusalem and Gaza,
eyes stream with tears,
as the prayers for the dead are chanted.

In India, on the streets of Mumbai,
beggars lift their hands
in the shadow of taxi cabs whisking visitors
from Germany and Holland on their way
to computer training
at the local technical university.

In the forests of Sarawak,
on the island of Borneo,
people who have never heard of Columbus, Ohio,
sing a new moon song.

And in Punta Arenas, Chile, the camera flashes
of tourists once again
scare shy penguins off the beach.

A typical week.
Flowers bloom
as the sky itself blooms over all of us.
Sorrow and joy, eating and mourning,
welcoming and learning,
foolishness and isolation.
A typical week
that comes to an end right now
in the heartbeat of this brief silence.


## IN HEAVEN

Ah, it's true.
When our ancestors spoke of heaven,
they were speaking of this moment.
When they went on about nirvana
they imagined a time like this.
When they sang of paradise,
it was this morning they imagined.
A time when all the mysteries of life and death
are blended in a community of praise,
when the bones of ancient lovers
are given flesh again in our own bodies,

teachers of long ago speaking of love and truth
once more in lives so ordinary they are
extraordinary.
Blest is our breath, in and out, quiet,
blest is our sitting, our fidgeting, our movement,
blest is our heartbeat echoing
the pounding alleluias of the distant stars,
blest is the silence that is presence,
not absence.


## PRAISESONG

O Mystery that everything exists!
I cannot name you!
I cannot say anything about you
that makes any final sense.
So I mostly keep quiet about you,
not even sure it's fair to say that you are a you.
Yet, nevertheless, even though you are nameless,
I am brimming with names
like a pitcher overflowing
with refreshing water:
friend, brother, sister, neighbor, foe,
maple, chrysanthemum, spruce, oak, palm,
sourdough, cabernet, artichoke, clams,
sparrow, cod, aria, table, carpet, quilt, soil, oxygen,
spark, ocean, and all the stars:

Mizar, Deneb, Delta Centauri and far, far Altair.
A thousand names, a million,
     all fleeting, all walking the precipice of time
     with me, all changing, becoming,
     sharing with you, who also becomes,
     the wholeness that is creation.
So blest are you, indeed, nameless Mystery.
Before you, I will keep silent.
But just as blest is each and every thing
which has a name.
So again, I keep silence.


## LOVE PRAYER

Love, you are strong as a dark blue mountain.
Love, you are as fluid as a wide silver river.
Love, you are as splendid as clear night sky.
Love, you are as mysterious as a dark forest.
Love, you are as wise as enduring friendship.
Love, you are true power, not mere distraction
truth, not deceit,
purpose, not impulse,
poetry, not prose,
sing not sang,
now more than tomorrow,
but tomorrow more than yesterday.
Love, condense yourself into this moment,

permeate the silence that joins us in community,
so that in the fire of the words to come,
the promises of this hour
might be sealed in peace. Amen.

## A KOL NIDREI

Let's set it all down, you and me.
The disappointments.
Little and large.
The frustrations.
Let's open our fists and drop them.
The useless waiting.
The obsession with what we cannot have.
The focus on foolish things.
The pin-wheeling worry which wears us out.
The fretting.
Let's throw them down.
The comparisons of ourselves with others.
The competition, as if Domination
was the best name we could give to God.
The cynical assumptions.
The unspoken, shelved anger.
Let's toss them.
The inarticulate suspicions.
The self-doubt.

The pre-emptive self-dumping.
The numbing bouts of self-pity.
Let's sink them all like stones.
Like stones in the pool of this gift of silence.
Let's drop them like hot rocks
into the cool silence.
And when they're gone,
let's lay back gently, and float,
float on the calm surface of the silence.
Let's be supported in this still cradle
of the world, new-born, ready for anything.


## Mystical Song

Come my way,
a way that takes me
past all my escape routes,
a way shadowed by mountains serenely
floating overhead, and with
flattened molehills all around me.
Come my truth,
a truth that has no loopholes
or moth-holes, or frayed edges.
A truth as exciting as fire, and as bright—
as powerful as water, and as fluid—
as solid as earth, but as transparent as air.

Come my life,
a life that devotes itself to love,
a life that coaxes,
and ungums the works,
and gets me to waltzing on the hot coals
of my amazement.
A life that precedes all words of my mouth,
and survives them into silence.


## Bellsound

Quiet as a maple branch, black against the sky.
Quiet as a pond, frozen past the cracking.
Quiet as a head bundled up against the cold.
Quiet as the moment we slip into sleep.
Quiet as a room when all the guests have left.
Quiet as a snowflake falling on the tongue.
Quiet as a babe at breast.
Quiet as a friend bowing to a friend.
Quiet as a wren gliding over the park.
Quiet as everything within the widening round of
this bellsound.

## First Principles

There are red rocks in the Gobi desert
I will never see,
and blue waves near the Seychelles Islands
I will never gaze upon.
Songs are now being sung in a café in Singapore
which will never dance in my heart.
Rice cakes eaten yesterday by Ainu grandmothers
on the northernmost island of Japan
will never cross my lips.
The earthy scent of the dark mushrooms
growing in some of the forests of the Andes will
never melt on my tongue.
The texture of Van Gogh's painting
the Potato Eaters, in Amsterdam, will never
be rough under my roving fingertips.
My feet will never walk over Superbowl fields.
My sigh will never be heard at the North Pole.
The world is mostly outside me.
It's bigger than I am, greater than I am.
It's unaware of me speaking here,
and I will never know more than a million millionth
part of it.
I am simply me.
And others are who they are.
And together, each of us,
small fragments of a great whole,
make the world.

But, no one is really alone, even if they feel lonely.
All of us are together, different,
yet woven intricately into the whole.
Each one, a facet of reality, no more.
Each one, important, and no less.
Come, silence, and bless us
with a sense of our intrinsic worth.

## CREATION STORY

Dying stars condensed themselves
into stardust once.
And stardust condensed itself
into the elements of earth.
The elements of earth condensed themselves
into living cells.
Living cells condensed themselves
into organisms that swam and crawled on land,
then thundered through the trees.
Organisms that were great in size
condensed themselves into creatures
fleet of foot and deft of mind,
who could gaze at the faint stars and wonder
if the light was their father,
if the nourishing earth embracing them
was their mother.

These quick creatures, small and uncertain,
then condensed their human lives
of honest struggle
into lives of conquest and violence.
Little by little, a few human hearts
condensed themselves smaller
than those vast crowds around them
who clamored for power,
and gave power up for the burden of love
given freely to all their brothers and sisters,
even the hurt and the loud and the sad.
Then these few amazing hearts
condensed their saving insight
into the Word: "Love one another.
Love your neighbor as your self.
Know yourself and love yourself.
Receive the Love that embraces us all."
And then those words condensed themselves
even further,
into this small, small jewel of silence,
that sums the whole evolution of creation with the
elegance and honesty of wordlessness.

## An Irony for Public Worship

Funny how the sun never asks
about what I did or didn't do today before it sets.
Funny how the rain refuses to question my motives
before it soaks me through.
Strange how the peach is sweet in my mouth
whether or not I am feeling sweet that day.
Odd how the sky maintains its altitude
even when I am asleep, and not noticing.
Or how a toothache hurts even though
I passed all my tests and established a career.
Hard to express how the children in Sudan
mean the same thing when they say "I am" that I do,
even though we speak different languages,
and they will live a much shorter life than I will.
Difficult to comprehend how both music and silence
can seal the deal,
especially since no one spent even a single minute
composing the silence.


## T'hillah

*Barukh atah, Emeth!*
Blest are you, o Truth.
Like the fabled Moses,
I too can never claim to have seen you

"face to face."

Too often, I've hung my own face on you
and pretended that I know something I do not.
Indeed, my most honest heart confesses
that at most,
I have only caught the briefest glimpse of you
at the very edge of my eye,
and only when I get out of my own way,
my own rush, my own fury.

I sense your cool shadow on me
when I grow hot from the tears
I've been holding back,
or when I notice the sadness or whimsy
hiding in the silent eyes of those around me.

I sense your closeness when I gaze
at a star suddenly unveiled by a toreador cloud,
or catch at an early yellowness
in the leaves of the oak.

It's then I feel a brush of wings nearby,
and realize that I am a only a small part of it all.
Then I know that I am not the
great high power of the world,
but only a puff of breath hidden amid the
mighty blasts of the great whirlwind
called the universe.
Like a lacewing barely floating

on the tip of a small blade of green grass is my life
from beginning to end, a short footnote to
a vast essay of stars and space unbounded,
an essay neither signed nor finally symbolic.
And yet this truth, your truth,
is no sadness, but a joy,
no lack but a blessing,
like the sight of a child at play,
totally absorbed in the moment, and glad.
Blest are you, O Truth, who plays in this silence
like a child in the waves of an infinite sea.
*Barukh atah, Emeth.*


## EARTH

This is our earth.
It falls through heaven like a pearl
in a glass of plum wine.
There are no other earths that I know of.
There are no other skies that we have mapped.
This is our earth.
The Oneness who gave birth to it
remains nameless.
There was no midwife then
to bring us word of the birth-cry.
We only rejoice that it is.

This is our earth.
Ice caps its head. Glaciers clasp its feet.
Warm wind, like the breath of a lover,
breathes around its breast.
Mountains thrust up to the clouds, bringing joy.
Storms blow across its shores, bringing fear.
Silvery fish capture sunlight and haul it down
into the deep, as on shore, valleys spread
with ripening fruit. Cities teem with the
poor and disenfranchised in the shadow of
golden towers. Children live and also die.
Highways throb. Monks sit in silence. Mothers
work. Crickets chirp. Teachers plan. Engineers
design. Fathers write letters.
People marry
with and without the blessings of law.
People cry.
They laugh, and brood, and worry and wait.
This is our earth.
There are no other earths.
Before its wonder, philosophers fall silent.
Before its mystery,
poets admit their words are shadow, not light.
And all the great names religious teachers
have left to us
Ishtar, Shekinah, Terra Mater, Suchness, Wakan
Tanka, Gaia

suddenly refuse to announce themselves.
And so we too fall silent,
entering the time where words end
and reality begins.


## Communion Circle

The earth.
One planet.
Round, global,
so that when you trace its shape
with your finger,
you end up where you started. It's one. It's whole.
All the dotted lines we draw on our maps
of this globe are just that, dotted lines.
They smear easily.
Oceans can be crossed.
Mountains can be crossed.
Even the desert can be crossed.
The grain that grows on one side of the border
tastes just as good as the grain on the other side.
Moreover, bread made from rice is just as nourishing
to body and spirit as bread made from corn,
or spelt or teff or wheat or barley.
There is no superior land, no chosen site,
no divine destiny falling on any one nation
who draws those dotted lines just so.

There is only one earth we all share,
we, the living, with all else that lives
and does not live. Virus, granite, wave,
city, cornfield, prophet, beggar, child,
slum, tower, mine, robin, eel, grandfather,
rose, olive branch, bayonet, and this poem
and moment are all within the circle,
undivided by dotted lines or final certainties.
Everything,
everything, for good or ill,
is part of the shared whole:
sky, earth, song, words and now, this silence.

## Part as Parcel

I am part of you, O Truth Unfolding.
I am part of you.
I am part of a cosmos.
I cannot see
either its edge or its end.
How amazing!
I am part of a galaxy of a million, billion stars.
They say it's a pinwheel.
How wonderful!
I am part of a system of planets that swing
around a small parent star. How strong the hands
of invisible gravity must be

to hold it all together, just so!
I am part of a planet, green and blue,
along with mountains and seas,
sponges and spores,
lichen and lava,
robins and rain,
periwinkles and perch,
centipedes and cities.
How great the variety!
How astonishing the mutual dependence of it all!
I am part of a species
that belongs to a grouping of animals
called mammalia
and so is every other human being, equally so.
I am part of a political unit called a nation.
There are many nations,
each of them dear in many ways
to its local citizens.
I am part of a family with ethnicity, practice,
and love in the form of food,
rooted in the mountains of Emilia.
Others know other roots, other practices.
I am part of a circle of friends rooted,
not in ethnicity or food,
but in simple redemptive love.
I am part of a climate region,
part of a state,

part of a city,
part of a neighborhood,
part of a congregation,
and part of a staff.
And with you I am part and parcel of this moment,
this simple silence which lasts but a few breaths,
and then is gone forever.
But like cosmos, galaxy, planet, species, nation,
climate, city, neighborhood, family, and circles of
friendship, it is precious,
a present for which I give thanks.


## QUESTION PRAYER

What words would make it plain?
What oracle could put it just so?
What version of scripture could provide it?
Which science writer could find a metaphor
so compelling
that everyone at once would understand?
Which poet could turn a phrase quite that precisely?
Why should anyone wish that its meaning was
singular?
Why should anyone imagine that the final truth
must glow,
and illuminate into the deepest corners?

Why are the questions of those who live at ease
so different from those who live in constant struggle?
Why would anyone run away from the answers?
Why would anyone consider the necessary wonder
and practice of love
to be either a question or an answer?
Why is it that silence like this
brings both peace and unrest?


## ODE TO SILENCE

You, silence, are the ground
on which we build the fragile sandcastles of our every
spoken word.
You, silence,
are quicksand where curses and cockiness and
arrogance find their end.
You, silence,
are the strand of beach we stroll where loneliness
turns into solitude,
and our small heartbeats join the much vaster
heartbeat of tide and wave.
You, silence,
are the hand in which the pearl of the universe,
grown around the painful grain of human suffering,
rests in heartbreaking beauty.

You, silence,
are the wide, bright delta into which
the river of this prayer fans out,
before it flows into the indigo Deep,
quiet, dark and lovely.
Come, Silence, fill this moment.


## Spiritual History

Let my body remember.
Let my hands and feet remember.
Let my breath remember
those who have come before me,
those who have come before us.
Didn't Muhammad wait quietly in his cave?
And didn't Jesus sigh silently by the blue lake?
And Guan Yin, didn't she sit in silence
thinking about what to do before doing it?
And what was Siddhartha the Buddha doing
anyway under that tree if not just sitting quietly?
And Susan B. Anthony, didn't she push back
from her desk, and take a breath now and then?
And Florence Nightingale, didn't she
put down her nurse's hat
and think silently about what to write
in her essay on mysticism before she actually wrote it?

And Sophia Fahs, didn't she stop telling
stories sometimes and just sit there?
And didn't Black Elk just notice the sunlight
glancing off his chair sometimes?
And Starhawk, does she only talk and write, or
does she too keep silence?
Let us remember them all with our bodies.
Let us remember them with the silence
they too knew.


## FOREVER TURNING

*For the earth, forever turning,*
as late summer breathes hot in Capetown
and cold cuts like a knife through Columbus;
*for the earth, forever turning,*
as men chant the Qur'an in Sfax, Tunisia, by night
and women chant coming of age songs
to their daughters in Kuching, Borneo, by day;
*for the earth, forever turning,*
as the galaxy of Andromeda drops through
heaven silently with no knowledge of us,
and a star explodes in Fornax anonymously;
*for the earth, forever turning,*
as the last word in a language you and I have never
heard drops off the lips of a dying woman

and as the first words are spoken by a child
when his hands learn French Sign;
*for the earth, forever turning,*
this, my call for peace,
this, my call for weighing grudges in a scale
balanced by galaxies and blue whales,
this, my call for a silence on earth
which is but a brief emblem of the peace to come.


## EVOLUTION

How beautiful that, from timeless emptiness,
from potential and possibility,
the universe opened like a lotus flower.
How beautiful that the stars whirled like dancers,
and galaxies spread their arms like dervishes
to a music no one could yet hear.
How beautiful that stones born in the womb
of space gathered themselves up in a ring around
the newborn sun and solidified into the vast globe
beneath the foundation of this building.
How beautiful that boiling seas yielded soft round
life at last, which thickened into spines and fins and
gaping mouths, which struggled to the land and
gazed up at the steady stars without knowledge.
How beautiful that scales stretched into feathers,

and eggs became pouches, became wombs,
which opened onto time and brought us forth
with a shout.
And how humbling the pages torn from the calendar
of joy and doom:
the crosses and chapel ceilings, the wars and
hospices, the knowledge and uncertainty,
the laughter and tears,
the solitude and terror and hope.
How surprising that we argue about mysteries,
pose unanswerable questions,
and pretend that we might one day be perfect,
or even find a faithful measure of perfection.
Oh Love most high and most deep,
the edge of our reaching and the limit of our sinking,
may this silence
sign for us all that we know,
really know, about the universe.


## QUERIES

And if the spring wind asks me,
"Which way are you going?"
what will be my answer?
And if the tulips,
which are radiant today
but will droop by next week,

ask me, "How will you mark our passing?"
what will be my answer?
And if the sun and clouds in their game
of hide and seek ask me,
"Why are you not joining us and playing too?"
what will be my answer?
And if I sit down in my chair,
and the silence comes to me, and asks me
"What is this world which stretches
out past these walls and windows
and goes on far, far past the horizon?
A gift? A puzzle? A home? A challenge?
A song? An elegant form of question?"
what will be my answer?

## CONVERSATION WITH AVINU MALKENU

King. Lord of Hosts. The Almighty.
On this day of turning,
I turn away from You, Great Mystery,
if those are the only clothes you can wear.
These words are worn,
like a thousand-year-old door sill
needing to be replaced
before people stumble over it,
or get splinters in their feet.
I'd rather keep things simple,

sort of every day.
Nothing special. No dramatic gestures.
No golden filigree or ancient candlesticks.
You know, like say I am buying some
groceries at the local store,
and the cashier says, "How are you today?"
without thinking, but I answer,
"Fine. Really fine.  How are you doing?"
and really want to know.
Or say I am walking down High St. downtown
and I meet a homeless man
standing there, looking down at his shoes,
and instead of walking right past, I say, "Hello,"
and I offer him half of the sandwich I just got
from the deli, and sit down and eat it with him
and ask him his name.
Or, say I have to have a difficult conversation with
someone who is very inflexible,
and I really want to avoid that conversation,
but I go have it anyway.
All these moments are holy songs, aren't they?
Real conversations with You
who are beyond all belief and unbelief,
beyond knowing or even unknowing.
Just around me all the time,
in ordinary things, like a human sigh,
or human tears, or human longing.
You are always in these simple things,

asking me to be real,
and not run away. Thanks.
*Barukh atah*, Blest are You,
Silent Mystery and Pulse of the World.


## THE ROSE OF HAFIZ

There is a garden
where the poet Hafiz strolls every morning,
especially this one.
Mirabai usually joins him; and Rumi of course.
But Audre Lorde is there too,
and Edna St. Vincent Millay
and Langston Hughes
and quite often Emily Dickinson.
Hafiz begins to speak,
opening the scripture of the leaves
and reciting: Today we are making *hegira*, our
pilgrimage to understanding.
The sun flaming in the sky is as round
as communion bread;
The pebbles on which we walk
are each one a new stone,
a new *kaaba*, fallen fresh from heaven.
That tree over there

is the very one under which the Buddha will sit today.
And those plum blossoms? The prayer pennants
fluttering above the monastery garden.

Then Hafiz walks over to the golden rose at the
center of the garden,
an astonishing blossom slowly opening in the light:
I'm not sure, he says.
Is this the door into the Golden Temple?
Or a Torah scroll being unrolled before us?
Or is it a skeptic's heart questioning everything?

In answer, the garden bees chant.
In answer, the dark blue irises
do some Fancy Dancing.
In answer, the grass bows.
In answer, the gong of the setting moon strikes itself.
And all the poets moving through the garden
keep this very silence.


## Simple Amidah

I open my mouth in astonishment.
Praises fall forth with my every breath.
I bless that I am not the first,
nor shall I be the last,
to wonder under the stars that everything is.
I bless that everything is,

and that I am part of it all.
I bless that no one has any final answers,
and that no name
can be the final name for ultimacy.
I bless that it's possible to let fresh insight
displace convention.
I bless that it will still be possible on my deathbed to
grow deeper.
I bless that only the painful work of forgiveness
allows for any real joy in this life.
I bless that what is fractured
still dares to dream of wholeness.
I bless that there is enough to go around
if we give, not grab.
I bless that distance
can usually give way to intimacy.
I bless that justice is only just
if it transforms me
as well as the world outside me.
I bless that the good
are not those who strive to do good,
but those who allow their hearts to be vulnerable
to the inherent dignity of others.
I bless that peace
can never be declared impossible,
even in the Middle East.
I bless that ruined cities and ruined lives
can often be rebuilt.

I bless that prayers like this
are not foolish incantations,
but invitations to bless, question, and praise
as often as possible.
I bless that there is no place in the whole universe
that is not as sacred as any temple.
I bless that my breathing
can be a kind of thanking.
I bless the peace that takes nourishment
at the breast of justice.
I bless that both singing and silence are possible.


## When to Speak, When to Keep Silence

When the machetes of injustice
tear apart the fabric of the nation and the world,
I speak up.
When the sunset resembles purple and orange vines
entwined like lovers,
I sigh in silence.
When the mud of deceptions and trickery
smear the mirror of public life,
I speak up.
When the moon rests like a thin slice of lemon
in the sparkling glass of morning,
I smile in silence.
When the insecure bully me,

or the greedy clutch at the common purse,
I speak up.
When a song lifts my soul aloft like a lark,
I swoon in silence.
When wars and rumors of wars destroy
the hopes and lives of children,
I speak up.
When I am overcome by the sheer reality
of a communion of life
connecting every woman, man and child
on this one world earth,
I give thanks in silence.
When I am restrained by systems of control,
manipulation, denial and duplicity,
I speak up.
When words cease,
the breath moves deep and slow,
and the inner and the outer are as one for a time,
I wonder in deep, deep silence.


## EVERYONE'S MEMORIAL DAY

I think of the young men and women
who live in harm's way, who hear gunshots
and wonder if their next heartbeat is their last.
I think of the teachers who ache for vacation,
the students who have stopped learning now.

I think of the folks distorted by their addictions,
fighting uphill battles, wandering the streets,
or the mazes of their lives.
I think of those I know and those I do not know
who are facing health problems . . . dizziness, or
ringing, or aches in joints.
I think of their bewilderment and fear.
I think of those who are out of work, or who
hate their jobs, or who wish they hadn't retired.
I think of those who love their work,
or work too much,
or who have too many irons in the fire.
I think of those who paint,
or sing, or dance, or write poetry,
and I think of those who are blocked in their art
and can't move forward.
I think of those who are highly structured,
and I think of those who are spontaneous,
and feel constrained by structure.
I think of those who think and those who respond
with feelings first and want to burst.
I think of those who know betrayal and
disappointment,
and I think of those who know
love and surprise and unexpected joy.
I think of the music to come.
But even before my first thought,
I am glad to welcome You, Silence, first.

APRIL

The symbols of the season
are all in place:
The sacred sift of morning light
through red-bud branches,
the drift of rain-clouds
sailing along the dark north sky
serving as a robe for a feast day,
the minarets of yellow tulips
ringing the call to prayer,
the young bees chanting their sunrise communion
service as they sip nectar
from the chalice of the narcissus flower,
the newly packaged seeds and burrs reciting
their Passover *maggid* of strange travels and quick
escapes on the wind.
Once again the tapestry of family dinners
and the peculiar loneliness of holidays.
Once again the jarring of murky world events
set against the soft pastel butterflies of spring.

Oh Love, the time is tender
and sweet here on the earth,
but the orbit of its passage is tough and jagged,
filled with sorrows that silence themselves.
Therefore come, Silence deeper than our
speechlessness,
rock us close in your silent arms for a while.

## Exultet for Easter Morning

I could say they are beautiful,
those stars hemming the blue veil of morning.
I could say it gives me pleasure,
that bronze and perfect Passover moon,
or I could say they make me glad,
those laughing daffodils along the lane.
Or, I could just as well say they are lit from within,
divine, overflowing with what some long to call
revelation, or even the growing vision of God.
But today, on Easter, I don't care which words I use to
express my wonder.
I just am glad to be alive, blest with such marvels.

I could say that the earth hanging in space
is an accident in the universe that just happened,
or I could say it's one more miracle
in a cosmos full of miracles,
one overflowing with divinity.
But today, on Easter,
for all of my education and life experience,
I cannot tell which word is which.
Accident. Miracle.
They seem to see each other's face
in the mirror of my heart.
And so I rise in gladness again,
and sing the marvel that everything is!

When some argue for heaven,
and others argue for earth,
for the life of me I cannot comprehend the
seriousness of the debate.
After all, the heaven I see daily overhead
never argues with me.
It just tumbles clouds through my eyes and yours
and paints the horizons pink and orange
come evening or come morning.
And the earth I walk never argues with me either.
It mostly just explodes with buds and petals
like some out-of-control fountain.
Heaven and earth remain silent even when people
malign the ancient exclamation "O God!"
by fusing it with violence and entitlement.
But now, on this Easter Day, everything grows
beyond words, beyond earth and heaven, into
a necessary vision of harmony and peace for all
humankind who rise into life that is alive.


## SPRING BENEDICITE

Splendors of the spring world,
uplift me.
Peonies, you slow-motion fireworks,
beguile me.

Sunday sky, the color of a newborn's eyes,
regard me.
Starry night, the color of opals strewn across rain-
soaked earth,
enchant me.
Fields of spring, sweetening the air,
calm me.
Glory of iris, pulsing in my pupil like the warm blood
in my wrist,
astound me.
All you realities of the spring world,
call to me.
Man on the street corner talking to himself,
beguile me
no less than peonies.
Woman recovering slowly from deep hurt,
move me
no less than the expanse of the sky.
Child without either shoes or good guidance,
teach me.
All you parts of nature, human and floral,
elemental and mysterious,
silence me.

## AUGUST

The chicory flowers
are grabbing pieces of the blue sky again,
and anchoring them onto earth
so we can marvel up close.
The dignitaries have returned home
to the capital, but the robins are still here locally,
as well as a handful of sparrows;
plenty of dignity there!
And the gothic arches of maple and oak
are exquisitely darkened by the week's rain.
O World, you never stop,
you always astonish,
you hold nothing back!
What can I offer you in thanks
but a small portion of the Silence
that once gave birth to you,
as once you gave birth to me.


## SUMMER SILENCE

In summer,
I do not come to worship
so much as worship comes to me.
In the morning, golden light splashes across
my rooms, and roses the color of wine

greet me in the alley.
As they bow to me in the breeze, I bow back.
At noon, sunflowers refuse to turn their face from me
until again I give a slight bow.
What else was I to do?
In the evening, the thunderheads
mount higher and higher,
gathering pink and rose from the setting sun,
creating the kind of vast mountain
hanging suspended in the air,
the very mountain Jesus spoke of,
or the Sufi poet Rumi
or Krishna's wild lover, Mirabai.
Again, I pause and bow. What else can I do?
At night, when the pastel sky melts
into a dark indigo lake overhead,
the rusty beacon of Mars
beckons above the horizon,
so that I cannot fail to notice and bend the knee.
My friend Richard calls me from San Francisco
or Doug e-mails me from Paris,
or Kevin leaves a voice message,
and again, I am bending and bowing in thanks.
The bows are small gestures, I know,
but surely better than all these ineffective words.
And so in the end,
my praise turns to silence,
and silence turns to me.

## Early October

The Tree of Life,
of which we in this room
are but one small branch,
has many branches.
One branch bears those millions who celebrate the
birth of Mahatma Gandhi this week.
They are chastened by his challenge
to fight fiercely for the truth of things,
but without violence of any kind.
One branch supports those
who feel the strange joyful-sadness
that companions the yearly change
of green leaves into gold.
One branch offers nests for those who are pouring
over their lives, looking
at where they leave off and where they begin,
in preparation for the Day of Atonement.
A few branches grow toward those
who are facing troubles of mind or body,
and another few branches support those who
laugh with new love.
And the great trunk from which the branches lift,
ringed with its history of struggles and triumphs,
sends its roots deep into the earth.
The Tree of Life has many branches.
And I say, all of us are part of that one tree.
as the tree itself is part of the earth,

as the earth is part of the sun's family,
as the sun is part of our galaxy of stars.
as our galaxy is part of the universe,
and as the universe nestles
in the nameless womb
of primordial silence
that holds us all.


## ELECTION PROMISES

I hear the polls
are going to be open on Tuesday.
All day.
Good. I certainly intend to go to them.
I certainly invite you to go to them and vote too.
But today I say the polls
are not just open on Tuesday.
I say they are open every day.
Every hour. Even here. Even now.
Right now I am going to vote
for the robin's egg sky,
the vanilla clouds,
the purple shadow spreading
under the ginkgo tree,
I am going to vote for tulips and redbuds.
I am going to vote for love
that does not have

to run in someone else's circles
in order to be love.
I'm going to vote the homeless into homes.
I'm going to vote the uneducated into classrooms
that teach them in the way they learn best,
not the way that would be most convenient
I'm going to vote the sick into healing.
I'm going to vote the lost into belonging.
I'm going to vote, right now,
for the right to dream of a world
where the word politics
doesn't stop me in my tracks,
and where the word honor still
has a few good meanings left.
I'm going to vote right now
for the power of free people
to actually be free,
no matter who they are,
no matter who has abandoned them,
no matter who hates them.
I actually am going to vote for love,
I am going to vote for truthfulness as the norm,
not the exception.
I'm going to vote for a world
that doesn't vote for killing, control and swagger,
I'm going to vote for you.
I'm going to vote for me.
Right now. Right here. Silently. But for real.

## Late Fall

Less light.
A time of rest for eyes weary of bright lights
competing for our attention.
Less light.
A time to focus carefully on things
that the spotlight has missed.
Less light. No need to squint.
Eyes wide and alive.
Less light.
No need to look frantically
for what we might be missing.
Eyes closed and breath steady.
Less light.
Ample time to see the slant sun of dawn
kindling dewy webs between bare wet branches.
Less light.
Ample time to see the setting sun turn rain clouds
into formations of flamingos.
Less light.
A blessing to all who never quite find time
to sit in the dark silence during the noisy summer.
Less light.
A reminder to all those who need help remembering
that few paths in this life are clearly lit.
Less light.

A time to notice shapes and textures as well as color.
Less light. A gift of the tilting earth.
Less light.
A gift, a blessing, a reminder,
and a time of opportunity.
Blessed are you, light that wanes.


## THANKSGIVING

Clogged airports and freeways and long lines,
the season's first snow flurries,
grocery stores thronged, beet greens
slapping over the edge of the stuffed cart,
lists and more lists, phone calls and phone tag,
extra chairs up from the basement,
tearing open the packages containing
Guest-At-Your-Table boxes down at the church,
worries about Aunt Ophelia
and how she'll behave this year,
fretting about what to say to cousin Jerry about his
obnoxious jokes,
bittersweet memories of grandma sitting at the table,
her eyes staring into your soul.
It must be Thanksgiving time.
But not yet, not yet.
First, this time. This time right now.

Silent time. No lines, no shoving, no jokes,
no phone calls, no planning.
Just silence.
Silence that was there before the earth
was first made round,
Silence that will be there past every ending.
Silence that dwells
in the heart of an apple,
like the seeds do.
Silence that draws out our surfeit.
Silence that is our surest communion
with the distant fluttering of stars.
Silence.


## Winter Sequence

Grey skies over my head,
throw yourselves like quilts over my busy life
and remind me to sit down and rest.
Stars of winter,
Orion's sash sparkling
across the heavens, remind me by your distance
that, compared to the infinity of the universe,
every single thing I struggle with on earth
is small, parochial and hardly universal in scope.
Great music of the season,
glowing with

angel-songs and filigreed with great mysteries,
remind me that my own birth,
like the births of all people in this room,
was no less mysterious
than that ancient and celebrated birth,
no less brimming with wonder,
for all children that come into the world
have lives as precious to them
as Jesus' life was to him.

So now come, Love greater than my longing,
silence greater than fatigue of tongues,
and haul my heart away from the undue frenzy of
the season, and bestow it to rest, proportion and
the haunting dark beauty of winter's long nights.

## CHRISTMAS EVENSONG

It's the deepest part of the night now.
Many mothers give birth this night
in Mexico, in New York City, in Kuala Lumpur;
in Sinkiang, China, and Talinn, Estonia.
Some are poor, some well to do.
Some call this time Christmas,
some do not.
The midnight in Punta Arenas, Chile,
is scented with summer roses,

and groups of friends in Hobart, Tasmania,
gather for mint tea on the patio,
commenting on the beauty
of Christmas sunsets.
Some will never be mothers or fathers.
Some will.
Close to Irkutsk, in Siberia,
the dark ice of lake Baikal cracks,
while on the outskirts of Ulaan Bator, Mongolia,
children who have never heard of either Jesus or
candles dream of riding horses over the hills.
Over Montevideo, the Southern Cross rises
bright among the constellations
as midnight yields its ancient Spanish carols.
Over Montreal, Orion hovers,
it's belt a comforting sash across the icy-cold sky.
A new mother sees the stars from her hospital bed
and smiles.
The world is great, the world is glorious
and this wondrous night
tells only one small part of its story.
Yet I say even this part of the story is great.
And each word in the story is great.
And the breath of silence between each word,
and the silence found
at both the beginning and the end of this story
is an emblem of a greatness and glory
yet to be discovered.

# III ELEGIES

## Morning Psalm

O You who may not even be a You,
I often find it hard to pray.
I suppose part of it is that
I really don't imagine that You
are some sort of Santa Claus in the sky,
and frankly, I hate to ask for things anyway.
I've always been independent.
I'd rather You just pour Yourself
into my life and ailing body
without me having to ask for it.
I'd like to be free to move my side again,
and toss the limitations that dog my tracks.
I'd like to be able to walk again easily,
and read without strain.
The most vivid part of me wants my health back,
my capacity for self-care.
I'd like to sit with my head held high

in the fresh air of morning.
I'd like to have long talks with Diene
about life and love,
long talks where I say everything
I have ever wanted to say.
But I just don't know for sure
how this prayer might work
to help me in that regard,
or even if it works,
in any ordinary meaning of that word.
I have had enough disappointments
in my life to want to face any more.
So you'll understand if I am a bit hesitant
around prayer.
But I guess it's worth the price of admission
just to be able to say clearly what I want.
So with that, I'll sign off for now,
and get on with the day ahead of me.

## EVENING PSALM

O Love Most High, Most Deep, Most Abundant,
as I lie here in my bed,
I think about the day.
Just today. Not past days.
I do not think much about tomorrow

either, for that is still many precious
moments away from now,
and now is when You live and I live.
The homestead of tomorrow has not yet been built
from the sod of today's memories.
For a while, at least, I yield my disappointment
that I cannot know what part of the future I shall
know, the future of my life and my family's lives.
I do not know if I shall see their hair frost with age
or no.
I do not imagine anymore I shall dance
at my great-granddaughter's wedding.
And so I turn to the unmistakable reality of this
room, with its walls, its sheets on the bed,
its chairs and note cards.
Here is the world of my life,
the edges of my dominion for a time.
The night shall drift into my eyes
as it has so many other nights. And in my dreams,
those gifts that give the finite a feeling of forever,
I can walk, and maybe even fly a bit
like a crow leaping from a fence-post.
Thank you for the gift of this moment.
Yesterday and tomorrow are, after all,
but poor angels who can only attend
to the bright divinity of this very second.
Come, sleep with me, O Love,
and soothe me with burdenless rest.

## Psalm to God

O God, sometimes the antique word of Your name
still brings comfort.
I know that many have used it
to curse, to bolster up their excuses
for violence and harm,
but I also remember
that some have walked with the mystery
without embarrassment,
shaping a sweeter image of You,
by reaching out to the sick, or embracing the poor,
or writing a poem that heals hearts.
O God, now however, I want an angry You.
I cannot but spill over, and cry out with rage,
"Cut the coils of the stroke that binds me,
loosen the cords of my tongue
by the sharp knife of Your impossibility.
Unbind my body with muscles
fashioned by your impatience."
And, if this is not possible,
then let your arms hold me close
in my dreams, in my inward imaginings,
the very parts of me that most resemble You.
Hold me close; let me sense not
my alienation from the Great Mystery of this life,
but rather, let me sense my intimacy with You,
the Greater Mystery that Anything Is At All.

O comfort me with family, friends and tears,
turn me toward the best part of me,
and bid me let up on myself a bit,
and love myself more than I do.
O God, I say now one of your most ancient names
as I pray:
Come, O Love, and fill this moment. Amen.


## GLORIA

Glory be to You,
Great Mystery of All!
I remember the brightness
of every star I ever saw,
and know that my remembrance
and every flash of light
shed by those distant miracles proclaims the Glory,
no matter my words,
no matter my silence,
no matter my belief or unbelief.
Glory be to You,
Unity binding all things,
source of my link to star, stone and starfish;
source of my link to song and solace.
You tether me
to wild Jesus and Buddha

and Dan O'Neal gone before me,
to my great-grandparents gone before me,
to my great-great-grandchildren, not yet born,
to the great-godchildren of my mentoring years,
children not yet even imagined.
You link all that has ever been,
is or will be in a great mystery named Harry.
Therefore, glory be to You,
Universal Love, in *excelsis et in terra*!
Even when I have been hard on myself,
family and friends still come.
Even when I doubt myself,
and my patience falters with my hope,
they arrive.
Even when all that befalls me now
fills me with a thousand things
I have no power to express, still they come,
and still my own heart
fills with loving-kindness for all.
*Gloria tibi, Amor in excelsis et in terra!*


## LAUD FOR LIFE

O Gift of Life,
I open you, on this my birthday,
when, like every day,
I am born anew in the recognition that life is,

and I know that it's for me.
I tear off the gaudy wrapper of expectation
around you,
and rip off the ribbon of resentment.
I unfold the box,
and find therein the best memories
of my childhood: that dark crow,
my deep sorrows,
my chaplain years filled with prayers,
my loving and marriage, my ministries,
my self-exploration on the couch,
my parenting, my joy and my grief, my new marriage,
my family and friends gathering round, the poets
gathering round,
my present fight against all that befalls me now.
And I hold these gifts up to your light,
O Sun of Life
like a handful of jewels blessed with many facets.
Your light is so bright that if there are any cracks in
the jewel,
any fragility, any cloudiness,
I cannot see them now.
O Gift of Life, full of caprice
and strange surprises, I say it clearly.
Even in this miserable bed,
I am alive like all who are alive.
And great is the sum of the gifts
given me and to all people.

I will never turn from this gift of life,
accepting every moment of it
until the time comes when the gift
no longer opens. But that time is not now.
Nameless source of Life!
Ah, I am still astonished that I live
Thank you.


## THE HALLOWING OF THE SILENCE

The lights are coming, I know it.
In the dark silence of coming night,
they are coming, those constellations
by which the wise may safely steer.
I know I will lose myself in that beautiful silence,
and its unimaginable lights,
as I have for a moment lost myself in this prayer.
See? For the length of this sentence
at least, I forget my sorrow.
For the length of this sentence at least,
I yield all my fears and loneliness.
The silent night is coming
with bright lights I still cannot see,
for it is day yet, and even in this bed
I have not lost the power to be amazed
by the glory of the day.

But as there is more delight, I hear,
more awe, more sheer amazement
under the dome of night's heaven
than in the glaring, blinding, too-busy day,
so let it also be
for my own personal night of the soul
that it shall one day yield more
guiding stars than the garish day
has ever given or even has power to reveal.
Let the majesty of those stars
melt me in the crucible of awe
that lifts me up from myself.
Pour me out like liquid silver
into a vessel most shaped like hope,
that I too might reflect all this light
that shines in the night,
and guides others on their way.
One day soon perhaps I too will become a star
that leads others in beauty and peace.
And now, for a time, I yield my fears, my sorrows,
and my daydreams to the night, silent and bright
and peaceful, yes,
peaceful, like the sound of crickets
in a wheat field bronzed by the moon,
where I might dream I recline on a quilt
under the summer stars at midnight,
drinking in the sweetness of it
all with a joy I never imagined possible.

The night is coming.
But the beauty of the stars
shall amend my fretting,
and restore me to the self
that is deeper than my days.


## BLESSINGS

Blessed is every breath I take.
Blessed is every fear I face.
Blessed is every robin's nest.
Blessed is every bough of spruce.
Blessed is every shell on the beach.
Blessed is the lap of the waves.
Blessed is the droop of a willow.
Blessed is the sweep of the prairie.
Blessed is the gable of my house.
Blessed are my family and friends.
Blessed is my love, the depth of my
strength which is deeper than
my present brokenness.
Blessed is the honesty of my fear,
and my fierce love of life;
Blessed is Love
that forever remembers my future,
and trembles with my tremors.

Blessed is the courage that I did not know I had.
Blessed is my desire that I might speak unfettered.
Blessed is the song of life
one of whose notes is me.
Blessed is the beauty of it all.
Blessed is my thanksgiving.
And blessed is my dream of peace for all those
I love, beginning with myself. Amen.

# IV  FINALE

## Solemn Te Deum for Peace

Can you imagine it?
Palestinians and Israelis settling down together
in their common lands
bound together by the silver covenant of Jordan,
marrying each other,
reading each other's books,
singing each other's songs, laughing?
Can you imagine it?
Afghani pilgrims in turbans and tunics,
women dressed with ancestral modesty,
coming to Al Quds to bow at the site
where Muhammad dreamt he leapt to heaven,
nearby joining their *sabra* friends
as *seder* guests?
Can you imagine Judith and Bill Kaufman
from Columbus, Ohio,
living on that court not far from Aladdin's

visiting their friends Omar and Fatima Al-Din
in Baghdad, their pink-cheeked children
joining in dancing till they're dizzy with joy
under the backyard fig-tree
while the grown-ups discuss the writings
of Iqbal over fried artichokes?
Can you imagine wide-eyed Cubans
from La Habana vacationing in LA or Miami?
And the other way around?
Can you hear it?
Tears lubricating the clatter of Spanish and
English into laughter,
no more the crack of ricochets
breaking the earshot of those who now
embrace shoulder to fleshy shoulder,
with hands stroking backs fiercely,
with deep and wracking sobs?
Can you imagine it? Really, can you see it?
The president of the United States
extending a hand the color of Ethiopian coffee
to sign her witness on the marriage certificate
of her daughter Charlene to her partner Chantal?
Can you imagine it?
Not saying "I have no money to give you today"
because no one has to ask?
Can you imagine not having to fret
about traveling here or going there,
or wanting to slink past the man in the tarry coat

asking for spare change?
Can you imagine childcare and soulcare as if
children and the spirit really mattered?
Can you imagine it?
Can you imagine healthcare by healers
instead of by insurance cartels?
Can you imagine no one lying to you
about their need for cocaine or Coors
because addiction and all of its sources
have been taken seriously?
Can you imagine no one calling sex
"dirty" or their foul moods "black"?
Can you imagine no one hiding behind
the safety of their guilt and blame?
Can you imagine it?
Can you imagine people not having to shout
because they are already heard,
or people going to work instead of overwork?
Can you imagine it?
When I fail to have this vision before
the eyes of my heart, daily, hourly,
written into my pulse and breath
tattooed in them as a saving text,
then come, Spirit,
Purveyor of Peace, Paz, Paix, Pace,
Friede, Salaam, Shalom, Mir,
You Reality beyond doubt,
Incandescent Nameless

No Thing at the center of all things,
and annoy me, burn in me, jar me, jostle me,
overcome me, shake me, startle me,
until I am willing to see what must be
even more clearly than I see what is.
And let me never be embarrassed by my vision,
nor ever again confounded.